VIOLA
78VA

All for STRINGS

COMPREHENSIVE STRING METHOD • BOOK 1
by Gerald E. Anderson and Robert S. Frost

Dear String Student:

Welcome to the wonderful world of orchestra music!

The moment you pick up your stringed instrument, you will begin an exciting adventure that is filled with challenges and rewards.

Using **ALL FOR STRINGS**, your teacher will help you to develop the skills that will enable you to become a fine string player. If you study carefully and practice regularly, you will quickly discover the joy and satisfaction of playing beautiful music for yourself, your family, your friends or a concert audience.

We hope that **ALL FOR STRINGS** will lead you toward many years of pleasure in beautiful music making.

Best wishes!

Gerald E. Anderson
Robert S. Frost

ISBN 0-8497-3223-9

kjos NEIL A. KJOS MUSIC COMPANY • SAN DIEGO, CALIFORNIA

LULEK

PARTS OF THE VIOLA

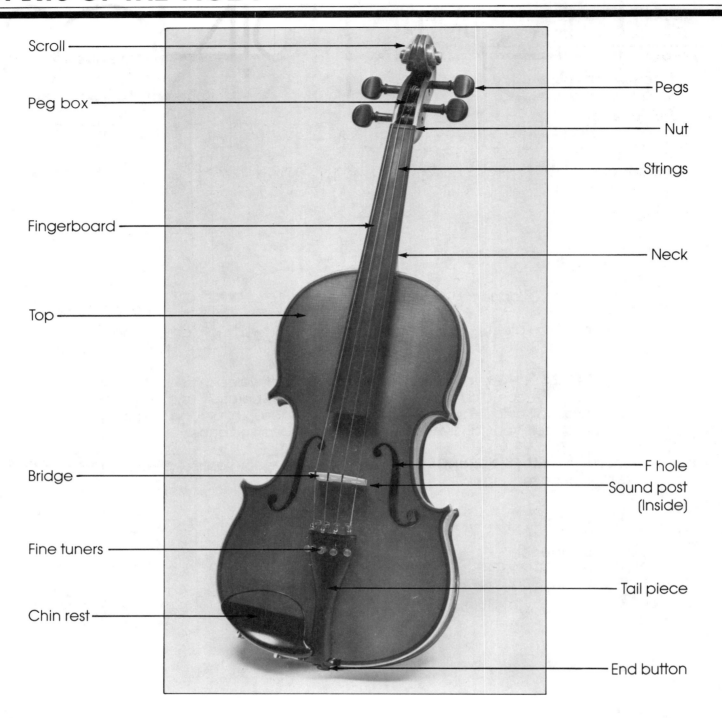

Scroll

Peg box

Fingerboard

Top

Bridge

Fine tuners

Chin rest

Pegs

Nut

Strings

Neck

F hole

Sound post (Inside)

Tail piece

End button

PARTS OF THE BOW

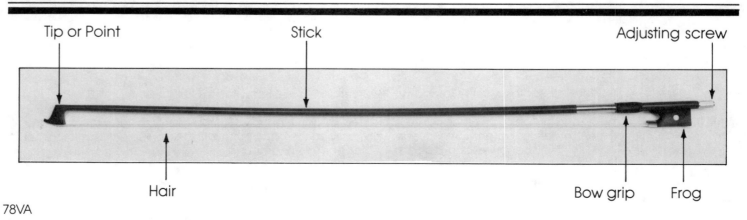

Tip or Point

Stick

Adjusting screw

Hair

Bow grip

Frog

CARE OF THE INSTRUMENT

1. Handle your instrument, bow and case with care. Instruments and bows are made of thin wood, and can break easily. Bumping your instrument, either in or out of the case, may cause it to go out of adjustment.
2. Keep your instrument clean. Each time you finish playing, use a soft cloth to wipe the rosin dust from your instrument, bow stick and strings.
3. When you are not using your instrument, always store it in its case.
4. Before placing your instrument in its case, remove the shoulder rest.
5. When your instrument is in the case, keep the case latched securely.
6. Never put your method book in your case. Placing your book in the case may cause your instrument to break or to go out of adjustment.
7. Do not expose your instrument to excessive heat or cold. Extreme temperatures may cause your instrument to crack.
8. Check your bridge often. If it is not standing straight, ask your teacher to adjust it. Do not adjust it yourself.
9. Do not attempt your own repairs. Only an expert musical instrument repairman has the skill and experience to repair your instrument.
10. Do not let others play your instrument.

CARE OF THE BOW

1. Be careful! Bows break easily. Do not drop your bow or hit it on anything that will cause it to break.
2. Do not touch the hair of your bow. Moisture, perspiration, oil or dirt from your hands, face, or hair will spoil the bow hair.
3. Before you begin to play, tighten your bow with the adjusting screw. Your teacher will show you the correct tension to use.
4. Each time you finish playing, loosen the tension of your bow. Your teacher will show you how much to loosen the bow hair.
5. When you are not using your bow, always store it in the case.
6. Rosin your bow several times each week.

ACCESSORIES

1. Rosin
2. Shoulder rest
3. Soft cloth
4. Extra set of strings
5. Music stand
6. Pitch pipe
7. Music folder

Figure 1

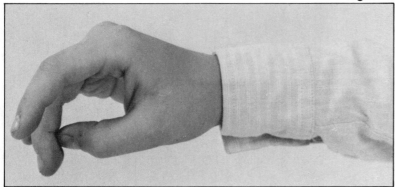

Figure 2

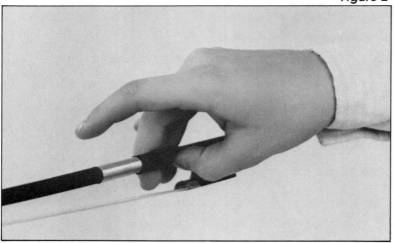

Figure 3

Figure 4

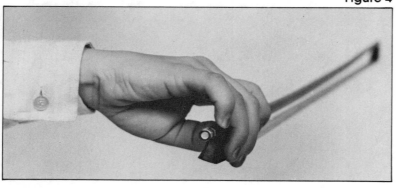

BOW GRIP

1. Make a **circle** with the tip of your thumb on the first joint or crease of your middle finger. **Keep your thumb bent.**
   See figure 1.
2. a. Holding the middle of your bow (pencil) with your left hand, lift your right hand thumb and place the stick (pencil) on the first joint or crease of your middle finger.
   b. Place the tip of the thumb on the stick next to the frog.
   Keep your circle.
   Keep your thumb bent.
   See figure 2.
3. a. Turn your hand inward or toward the tip of the bow.
   b. Place your index finger between the first and second joints over the stick (pencil).
   See figure 3.
4. Lay your ring finger comfortably over the stick (pencil) on the frog.
   See figure 3.
5. Place the tip of your little finger on the top of the stick (pencil).
   Keep your little finger curved.
   See figures 3 and 4.
6. Check your entire bow grip.
   Reminder: THUMB BENT
            LITTLE FINGER CURVED
            HAND RELAXED
   See figures 3 and 4.

BOWING

1. Place the bow on the string half way between the bridge and the fingerboard.
   See figures 5 and 6.
2. Tilt the bow stick slightly toward the fingerboard (away from the bridge).
   See figures 5 and 6.
3. Press the bow firmly into the string.
4. Move the bow in a straight line with the bridge. Keep the bow at right angles to the string.
5. Raise your wrist slightly at the frog and lower it as you draw closer to the tip.
6. Relax your right shoulder, elbow and wrist.

BOW GRIP EXERCISES

Your teacher will explain how to do these exercises.
1. Pinkie Lifter
2. Flex
3. Wave
4. Teeter-Totter
5. Squeeze-Relax
6. Windshield Wiper
7. Spider
8. Rocket Launch

Figure 5

INSTRUMENT POSITION ════════

1. Stand or sit with correct posture.
   See figures 5 and 6.

2. Attach the shoulder rest in the proper position on the viola.

3. Place the viola on your left shoulder.

4. Be sure that:
   a. your left shoulder is well under the viola.
   b. the left corner of your chin is in the chinrest so that you are looking straight down the strings.
   c. the viola is tilted slightly to the right.
   d. the viola is parallel to the floor.
   e. the following are in line:
      · nose
      · strings
      · left elbow
      · left foot

      See figures 5 and 6.

5. Relax your left shoulder.

LEFT HAND POSITION ════════

1. Place the first joint of your thumb on the neck.
   See figure 7.

2. Curve your fingers over the fingerboard.
   See figure 7.

3. Adjust your wrist and forearm to form a straight line.
   See figures 5 and 6.

4. Be sure that:
   a. your thumb is relaxed, straight and pointed upwards.
   b. your thumb and first finger are opposite each other.
   c. your wrist is straight.
   d. your fingernails are cut short.

5. Relax your left shoulder.

Figure 6

Figure 7

STARTING BY ROTE

THE BASICS

DOWN BOW	UP BOW	PIZZICATO
⊓	V	*pizz.*
Move the bow toward the tip.	Move the bow toward the frog.	Pluck the string with the index finger of your right hand.

INSTRUCTIONS

RHYTHM PATTERN	PIZZICATO	ARCO
Play the assigned Rhythm Pattern ONCE for each letter using pizzicato or arco.	1. Place your index finger (1st finger) on the correct string. 2. Place your thumb on the corner of the fingerboard. 3. Pull the string firmly to the side to produce a good ringing tone. 4. Check your right hand pizzicato position.	1. Place your bow at the correct string level. 2. Play in the middle of the bow. 3. Use a forearm stroke to PULL the bow. 4. Check your right hand bow grip often. 5. Play with a good ringing tone.

NEW NOTES

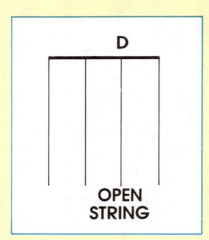

D

OPEN STRING

STRING LEVEL

Adjust your arm to play on the correct string.

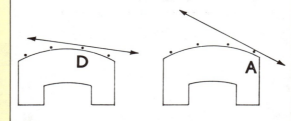

D   A

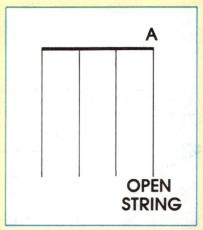

A

OPEN STRING

1. D STRING

| D | − :‖

2. TWO D's

| D | D | − :‖

★ Check your bow grip often.

3. A STRING

| A | − :‖

4. TWO A's

| A | A | − :‖

NEW IDEA

| PREPARE BOW | * | Go to the new string level. Be ready to play on the new string as soon as possible. |

5. D AND A

| D | − | A | − :‖

6. FAST PREPARATIONS

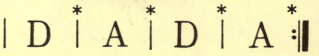

| D | A | D | A :‖

ARCO	MEASURE	WHOLE REST	REPEAT SIGN
arco			
Play with the bow.	bar lines	4 beats of silence	Repeat the previous section of music again.

RHYTHM PATTERNS

RHYTHM PATTERN #1

RHYTHM PATTERN #2

COMBINED PATTERN #1

NEW NOTE

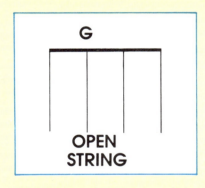 OPEN STRING

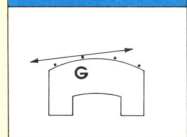 STRING LEVEL

7. G STRING
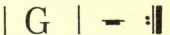

8. TWO G'S

★ Check your bow grip often.

9. G AND D

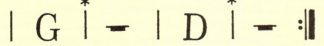
★ Is your right thumb bent?

10. FAST PREPARATIONS

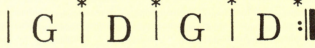
★ Roll the bow to a new string.

11. TWO TOGETHER
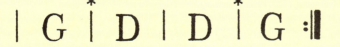

12. A DIFFERENT TWO
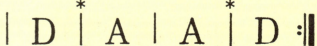

13. THREE STRINGS
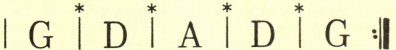
★ Be sure to use fast bow preparations.

78VA

NEW NOTE

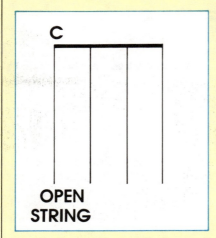

C

OPEN STRING

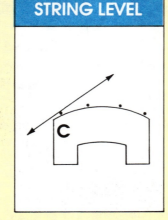

STRING LEVEL

C

14. C STRING

| C | – :‖

15. TWO TOGETHER

| C | C | – :‖

16. ALL FOUR STRINGS

| C | G | D | A | – :‖

★ Roll the bow to the new string.

17. A BIG JUMP

| G | – | A | – :‖

★ Check your bow grip often.

18. BIG PREPARATIONS

| G | A | D | C :‖

19. CIRCLE OF STRINGS

| C | G | D | A | – | A | D | G | C :‖

★ Be sure to use fast bow preparations.

MORE RHYTHM PATTERNS

RHYTHM PATTERN #3

ROS - IN

RHYTHM PATTERN #4

BOW

COMBINED PATTERN #2

ROS - IN   BOW

COMBINED PATTERN #3

BOW   ROS - IN

INSTRUCTIONS

Play all the preceding lines with these new rhythm patterns.

NEW NOTE

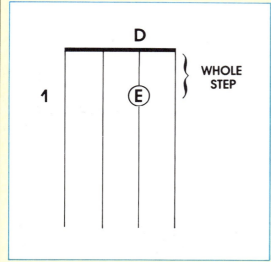

D

1   Ⓔ   } WHOLE STEP

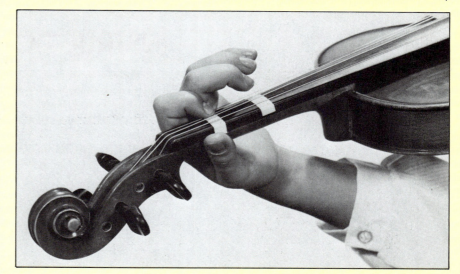

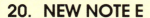

20. NEW NOTE E

| E | — :‖

★ Place your first finger on the D string.

21. UP TO E

| D | — | E | — :‖

★ Prepare your first finger during the rest.

22. PLAY TWO

| D | E | — :‖

★ Check the placement of your bow.

23. NO RESTS

| D | E | E | D :‖

NEW NOTE

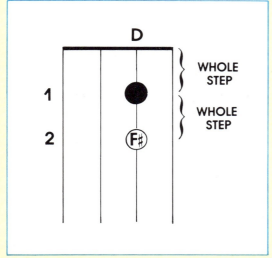

D

1   ● } WHOLE STEP

2   Ⓕ♯ } WHOLE STEP

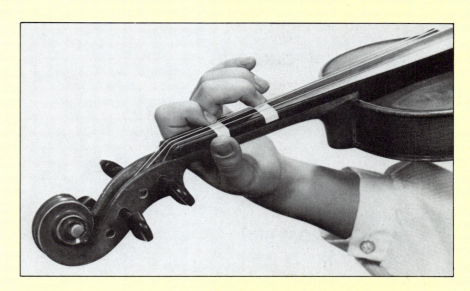

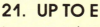

24. NEW NOTE F♯

| F♯ | — :‖

★ Place your first and second finger on the D string.

25. UP TO F♯

| D | — | E | — | F♯ | — :‖

★ Prepare each finger during the rest.

26. PLAY THREE

| D | E | F♯ | — :‖

★ Check your bow grip often.

27. STARTING ON F♯

| F♯ | E | D | — :‖

★ Prepare your fingers for F♯.

28. NO RESTS

| D | E | F♯ | F♯ | E | D :‖

★ Check your left hand position.

NEW IDEA

INSTRUCTIONS

The songs on this page are to be played in a different way.

1. Play one note for each letter. The letter with a line must be held longer.

2. The rhythm words appear under the letters of the first song. These rhythm words will guide you with the rhythm of the song.

3. The other three songs are familiar. If you do not know the songs your teacher will play them for you.

29. THREE NOTE MARCH

|D D D D |E E E ——— |F# F# F# F# |E E E ——— |
Mis - sis - sip - pi   Ros - in Bow ____ Mis - sis - sip - pi   Ros - in Bow ____

|D D D D |E E E ——— |F# F# E E |D D D ——— ‖
Mis - sis - sip - pi   Ros - in Bow ____   Ros - in   Ros - in   Ros - in Bow ____

30. FRENCH FOLK SONG

|D D D E |F# — E — |D F# E E |D ——— |
★ Is your right thumb bent?

|D D D E |F# — E — |D F# E E |D ——— ‖

31. HOT CROSS BUNS

|F# —— E —— |D ——————— |F# —— E —— |D ——————— |
★ Check your bow grip often.

|D D D D |E E E E |F# — E —— |D ——————— ‖

32. MARY HAD A LITTLE LAMB

|F# E D E |F# F# F# — |E E E — |F# F# F# — |
★ Check your left hand position.

|F# E D E |F# F# F# F# |E E F# E |D ——— ‖

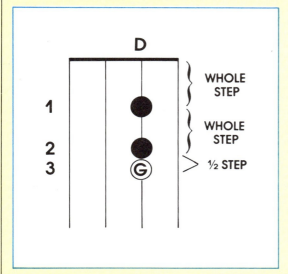

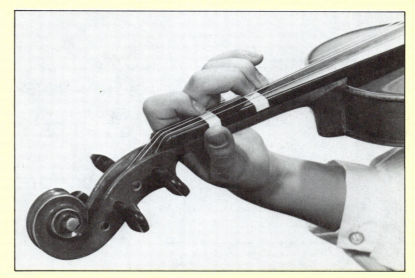

33. NEW NOTE G

| G | — :‖

★ Place your first, second and third finger on the D string.

34. GOING DOWN

| G | F♯ | E | D | — :‖

★ Prepare your fingers for G.

35. MOVIN' UP

| D | E | F♯ | G | G | F♯ | E | D :‖

36. ROSIN BOW MARCH

| D D D — | E E E — | F♯ F♯ G G | F♯ F♯ E — |

Ros - in Bow __ Ros - in Bow __ Ros - in Ros - in Ros - in Bow __

| D D D — | E E E — | F♯ F♯ G G | F♯ E D — ‖

★ Is your right thumb bent?

37. MARCHING SONG

| D D E E | F♯ F♯ G — | F♯ F♯ G G | F♯ F♯ E — |

| D D E E | F♯ F♯ G — | F♯ F♯ G G | F♯ E D — ‖

★ Check your left hand position.

38. CLIMBING UP

| D E F♯ — | E F♯ G — | F♯ G F♯ E | D D E — |

| D E F♯ — | E F♯ G — | F♯ G F♯ E | D E D — ‖

★ Check your bow grip often.

78VA

12

NEW NOTE

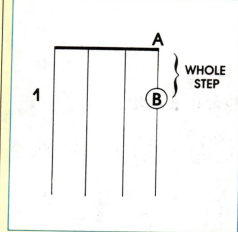

39. NEW NOTES A AND B

| A | B | A | B :‖

40. FOUR NOTES

| D | E * | A | B * :‖

NEW NOTE

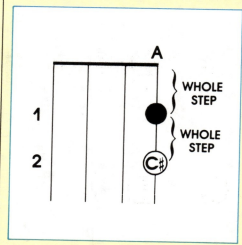

41. UP TO NEW NOTE C#

| A | B | C# | C# | B | A :‖

42. SIX NOTES

| D | E | F# * | A | B | C# * :‖

★ Roll the bow to the new string.

43. FRENCH FOLK SONG

| A   A   A   B | C# —— B —— | A   C# B   B | A ———— |

| A   A   A   B | C# —— B —— | A   C# B   B | A ———— ‖

★ Check your left hand position.

44. HOT CROSS BUNS

| C# —— B —— | A ———————— | C# —— B —— | A ——— |

| A   A   A   A | B   B   B   B | C# —— B —— | A ——— ‖

45. MARY HAD A LITTLE LAMB

| C# B   A   B | C# C# C# —— | B   B   B —— | C# C# C# — |

| C# B   A   B | C# C# C# C# | B   B   C# B | A ——————— ‖

★ Check your bow grip often.

8VA

NEW NOTE

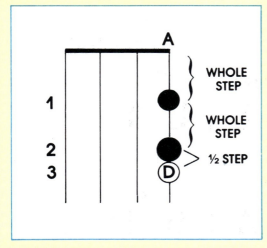

A

1

2
3

D

WHOLE STEP

WHOLE STEP

½ STEP

46. TO NEW NOTE D AND BACK

| A | B | C# | D | go on:

| D | C# | B | A :||

47. GOING UP THE D MAJOR SCALE

| D | E | F# | G* | A | B | C# | D* :||
open

★ Check your left hand position.

48. D MAJOR SCALE-UP AND DOWN

| D | E | F# | G* | A | B | C# | D |
open

| D | C# | B | A* | Prepare fingers on D E F# G |

| G | F# | E | D :||
open

49. Play **ROSIN BOW MARCH, MARCHING SONG** and **CLIMBING UP** on the A string.

50. TWINKLE, TWINKLE, LITTLE STAR

|D D* A A |B B A — |G* G F# F# |E E D — |
open

|D D* A A |B B A — |G* G F# F# |E E D — *|

|A A* G G |F# F# E — |A A* G G |F# F# E — |

|D D* A A |B B A — |G* G F# F# |E E D — ||

★ Check your bow grip often.

78VA

STARTING BY NOTE

THE BASICS

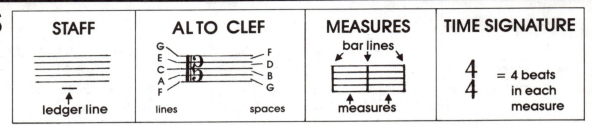

STAFF	ALTO CLEF	MEASURES	TIME SIGNATURE
ledger line	lines · spaces	bar lines · measures	$\frac{4}{4}$ = 4 beats in each measure

QUARTER NOTE	♩ = 1 beat
HALF NOTE	♩ = 2 beats

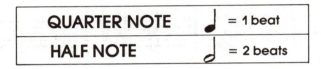

Counting	1	2	3	4
Alternate Counting				

NEW IDEA

STRING LEVEL	Adjust your right arm to play on the correct string.

NEW NOTES

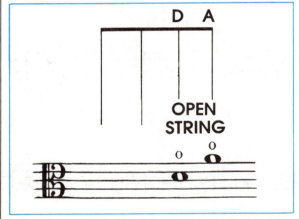

D   A

OPEN STRING

1. D STRING

2. A STRING

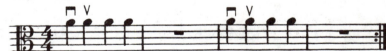

NEW IDEA

PREPARE BOW	*	Go to the new string level. Be ready to play on the new string as soon as possible.

3. D AND A

★ Check your bow grip often.

4. HALF NOTES

★ Move the bow slower for half notes.

WHOLE REST	REPEAT SIGN	DOWN BOW	UP BOW
= 4 beats of silence	Repeat the previous section of music again.	Move the bow toward the tip.	Move the bow toward the frog.

5. MISSISSIPPI RIVER

6. QUARTERS AND HALVES

★ Roll the bow to the new string.

7.

★ Be sure to use fast bow preparations.

8. ROSIN BOW

★ Is your right thumb bent?

9.

10. BOW ROSIN

11.

★ Check your bow grip often.

12. MIXING IT UP

★ Roll the bow to the new string.

NEW NOTE

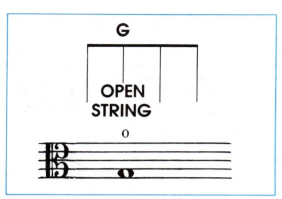

13. G STRING

14.

★ Check your bow grip often.

15. THREE STRINGS

★ Be sure to use fast bow preparations.

16.

NEW NOTE

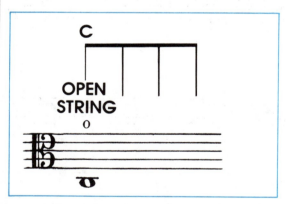

17. C AND E STRINGS

18. CIRCLE OF STRINGS

★ Raise and lower your arm to the correct level of bowing.

THEORY GAME

19. NAME GAME

★ Write in the note names.

20. MISSISSIPPI RIVER DUET

21. TRICKY BOWS

★ Play each section four times.   ★ Work for straight bowing.

22.

★ Be sure to use fast bow preparations.

23.

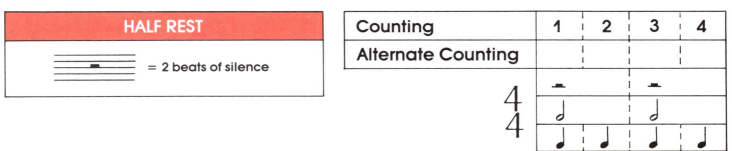

★ Is your right thumb bent?

NEW IDEA

HALF REST
= 2 beats of silence

Counting	1	2	3	4
Alternate Counting				

THEORY GAME

24.

★ Write in the counting.

25. OPEN STRING DUET

Also play this duet pizzicato.

78VA

NEW NOTE

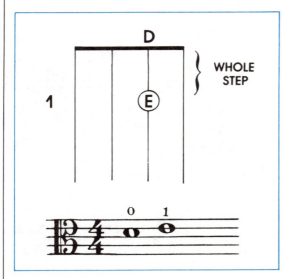

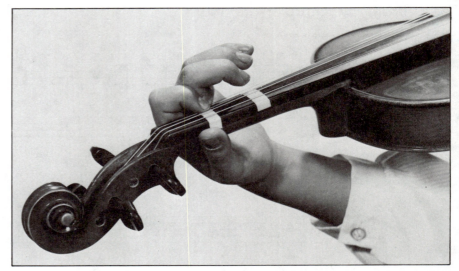

26. NEW NOTE E

★ Prepare your first finger during the rests.

27.

28.

★ Check your bow grip often.

29. FLASHY FIRST

30.

★ Keep your first finger down where indicated.

THEORY GAME

31. RHYTHM TEASER

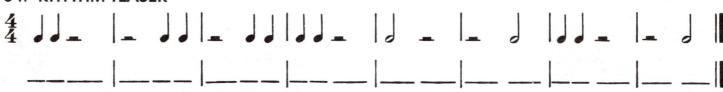

1. Write in the counting.   2. Clap and count.   3. Play arco or pizzicato.

NEW NOTE

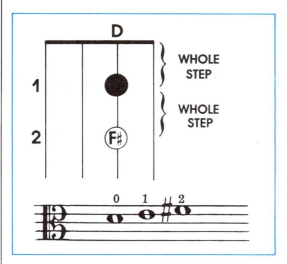

32. NEW NOTE F♯

★ Prepare the next finger during the rest.

33. KEEPING THE FIRST DOWN

★ Keep your first finger down when placing the second finger.

34.

35.

★ Keep your fingers arched above the string ready to play.

NEW IDEA

PREPARE FINGERS — To accurately play notes that involve a skip or an interval, put the finger(s) down on the notes between the interval or written notes.

36.

37.

★ Prepare your fingers between D and F♯.

38. MARY HAD A LITTLE LAMB

Traditional

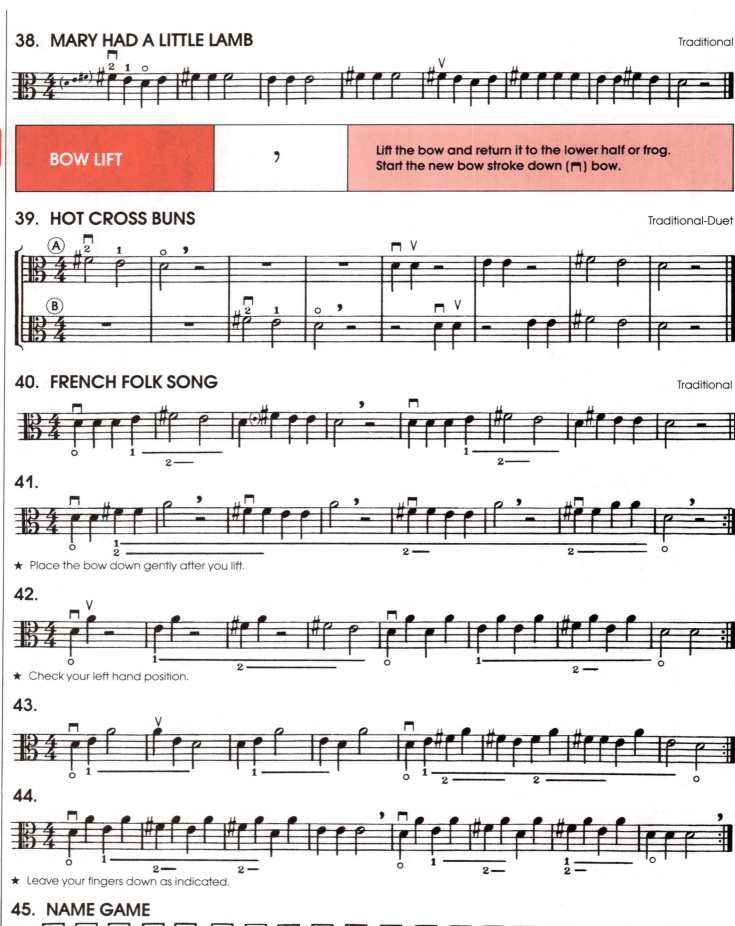

| BOW LIFT | , | Lift the bow and return it to the lower half or frog. Start the new bow stroke down (⊓) bow. |

NEW IDEA

39. HOT CROSS BUNS

Traditional-Duet

40. FRENCH FOLK SONG

Traditional

41.

★ Place the bow down gently after you lift.

42.

★ Check your left hand position.

43.

44.

★ Leave your fingers down as indicated.

45. NAME GAME

THEORY
GAME

★ Write the name of the line, space or note in the box at the end of each arrow.

NEW NOTE

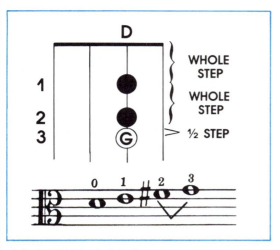

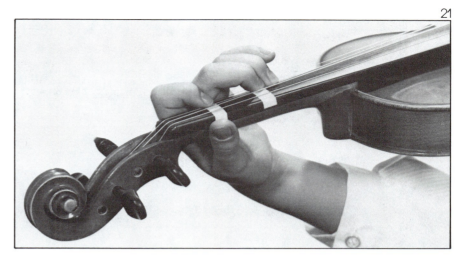

46. NEW NOTE G

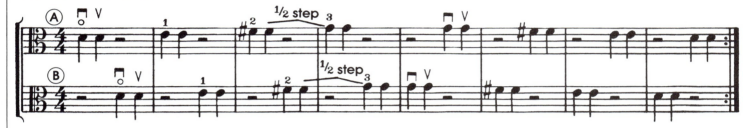

47. LEAVE FINGERS DOWN

48. MARCHING SONG

★ Check your bow grip often.

49. CLIMBING UP

★ Check your left hand position.

50. KEEPING FINGERS DOWN

51. ODE TO JOY

Beethoven

THEORY
GAME

52. NOTES AND NAMES

a g e ___ c a f e ___ b a d g e ___ d e f a c e d

★ Draw the notes as indicated in measures 1, 3, 5 and 7. Name the notes in measures 2, 4 and 6.

Counting	1	2	3	4
Alternate Counting				

53. COUNTING AND ANSWERS

54. RHYTHM TEASER

1. Write in the counting.   2. Clap and count.   3. Play arco or pizzicato.

55. SKIPS

56. MORE SKIPS

57. NORWEGIAN FOLK SONG

Traditional

★ Check your bow grip often.

58. DUET IN THIRDS

THEORY
GAME

59. RHYTHM TEASER

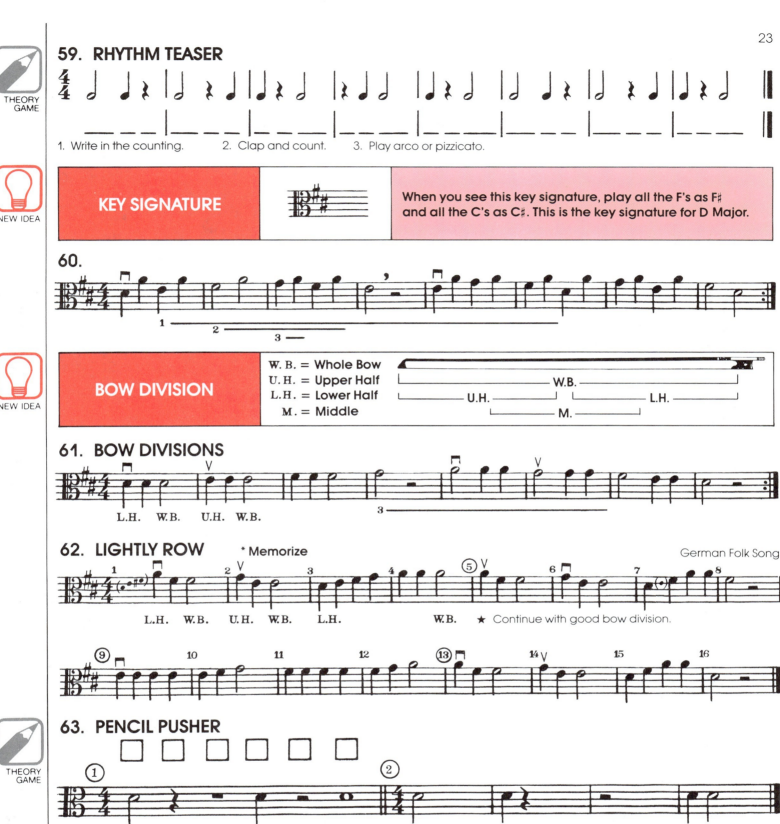

1. Write in the counting. 2. Clap and count. 3. Play arco or pizzicato.

NEW IDEA

KEY SIGNATURE — When you see this key signature, play all the F's as F♯ and all the C's as C♯. This is the key signature for D Major.

60.

NEW IDEA

BOW DIVISION

W. B. = Whole Bow
U. H. = Upper Half
L. H. = Lower Half
M. = Middle

61. BOW DIVISIONS

L.H. W.B. U.H. W.B.

62. LIGHTLY ROW   * Memorize

German Folk Song

L.H. W.B. U.H. W.B. L.H.   W.B.   ★ Continue with good bow division.

63. PENCIL PUSHER

① Write the number of counts each note or rest should receive in each box.
② Complete each measure with the correct number of half notes or quarter notes.

64. JINGLE BELLS

Pierpont

L.H. W.B. U.H. W.B.

★ Check the placement of your bow.

NEW
NOTES

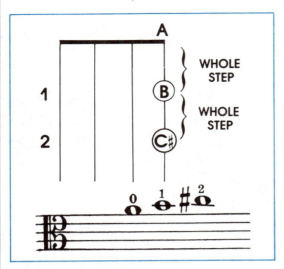

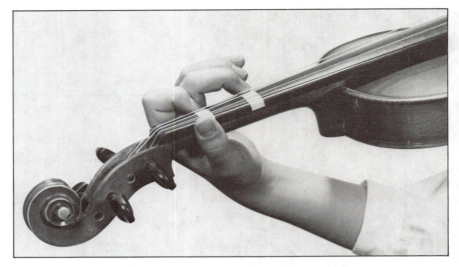

65. NEW NOTES B AND C♯

66.

THEORY
GAME

67.

★ Write in the note names.

68. FRENCH FOLK SONG

Traditional -Duet

69. LIFT SET GAME

Duet

★ Check your bow grip often.

NEW NOTE

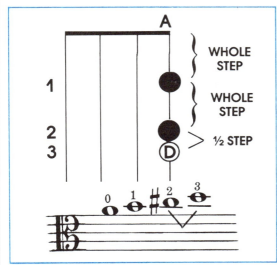

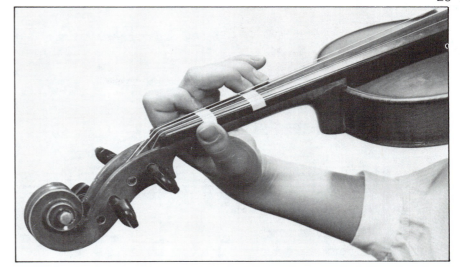

70. NEW NOTE D

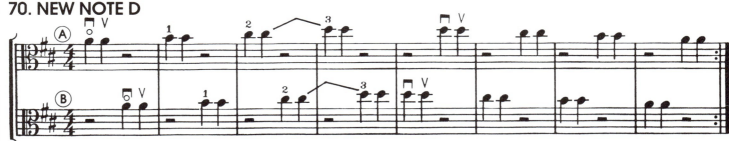

71. TETRACHORD MARCH

★ Refer to the inside front cover for the explanation of a tetrachord.

72. UP THE D MAJOR SCALE

★ Check your left hand position.

73. D SCALE ROUND

Round

★ Prepare the G in measure 6 coming down the scale.

74. DUET RHYTHMS FOR THE D MAJOR SCALE

A.  B.  C.  D.

NEW IDEA

SLURRED STACCATO BOWING	♩ ♩ or ♩♩♩♩ Also play 6-8-12-16 notes per bow.	This bowing is a series of *separated* notes played while the bow moves in one direction. Separate each note from the other.
LOURÉ BOWING	♩ ♩ or ♩♩♩♩ Also play 6-8-12-16 notes per bow.	This bowing is a series of *connected* notes played while the bow moves in one direction. Each note receives a distinct pulse. The bow does not stop but continues moving.

★ Play these bowings with the D Major scale.
★ Refer to page 48 for other bowing and scale possibilities.

78VA

💡 NEW IDEA

D.S. AL FINE	D.S. (Dal Segno) = sign *Fine* = finish	When you see the *D.S. al Fine*, go back to the 𝄋 (sign) and stop when you come to the *Fine*.

75. CONCERT SONG

Frost-Solo or Ensemble

★ Ensemble: A group of musicians playing different parts.

76. TECHNIC TRAINER NO. 1

77. TECHNIC TRAINER NO. 2

★ Roll the bow to the new string.

78. TECHNIC TRAINER NO. 3

★ Lift and set each finger carefully across to the next string.

79. TWO OF US

Duet

★ Check your bow grip often.

NEW IDEA

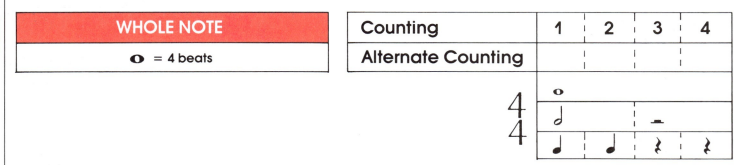

Counting	1	2	3	4
Alternate Counting				

WHOLE NOTE

𝅝 = 4 beats

80. SLOW BOWS

★ Draw the bow much slower for the 𝅝 (whole) note.

81. BOHEMIAN FOLK SONG

Round

★ Check your left hand position.

NEW IDEA

AABA FORM — The first musical section A is played two times, followed by a new section B. Then section A is repeated.

82. TWINKLE, TWINKLE, LITTLE STAR * Memorize

Mozart

83. PENCIL PUSHER

THEORY GAME

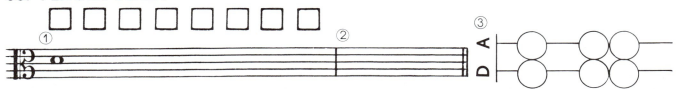

① Draw the notes on the staff to form a D Major scale. Be sure to include the ♯'s for the appropriate notes. Name each note in the boxes above.
② Draw your clef sign. Also add the key signature for D Major.
③ In the fingering chart above, write the name of the note that is played at the place of each circle.

NEW IDEA

| PICK-UP NOTES |  | Note or notes that come before the first full measure of a piece. Play single pick-up notes up (V) bow. |

84. O COME, LITTLE CHILDREN   * Memorize

Schultz

L.H.   W.B.   U.H.   W.B.   L.H.   U.H.   L.H.

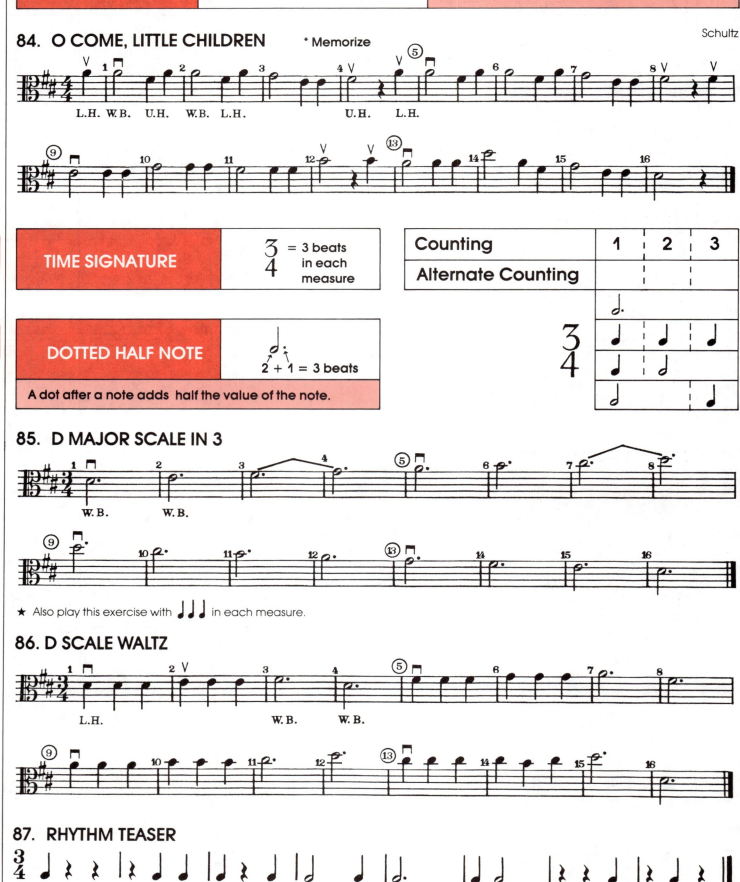

NEW IDEA

| TIME SIGNATURE | $\frac{3}{4}$ = 3 beats in each measure |

Counting	1	2	3
Alternate Counting			

NEW IDEA

| DOTTED HALF NOTE | 2 + 1 = 3 beats |

A dot after a note adds half the value of the note.

85. D MAJOR SCALE IN 3

W. B.   W. B.

★ Also play this exercise with ♩♩♩ in each measure.

86. D SCALE WALTZ

L.H.   W. B.   W. B.

THEORY GAME

87. RHYTHM TEASER

$\frac{3}{4}$

1. Write in the counting.   2. Clap and count.   3. Play arco or pizzicato.

88. POSITION CHECK

Right Hand	Left Hand	Playing Position
☐ Thumb bent	☐ Wrist straight	☐ Instrument held up
☐ Little finger curved	☐ Elbow under	☐ Sitting up properly
		☐ Straight bow stroke

Have your teacher check your position.   Place an X in the box for each item that is correct in your playing.

89. FRENCH FOLK SONG   * Memorize

Traditional

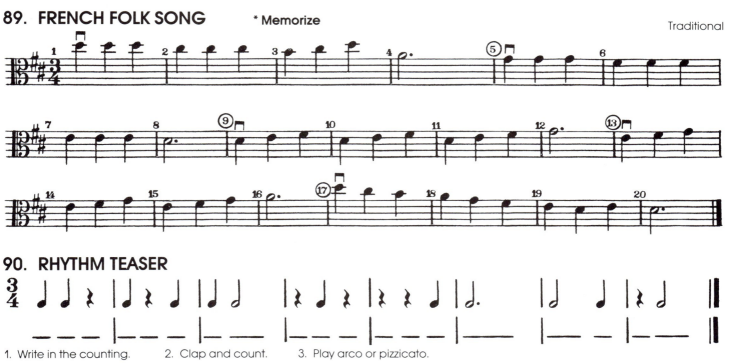

THEORY GAME

90. RHYTHM TEASER

1. Write in the counting.   2. Clap and count.   3. Play arco or pizzicato.

NEW IDEA

| D.C. AL FINE | *D.C.* (Da Capo) = beginning
Fine = finish | When you see the *D.C. al Fine*, go back to the beginning and stop when you come to the *Fine*. |

91. TRICKY MELODY

Fine

D.C. al Fine

★ Clap and count this melody before you play.

92. SCOTLAND'S BURNING

English Round

93. BALANCE THE SCALE

Write in notes or rests to balance each scale. Be sure that the notes or rests on one side of the scale balances with the notes or rests on the other side.

THEORY GAME

78VA

NEW IDEA

SLUR

A slur is a curved line that connects two or more notes of different pitches. Keep the bow moving and change the fingering for the second note. The sound should be smooth and continuous.

94.

★ To slur two notes, use half of the bow for each note.

95.

★ Also play this bowing pattern on the A string for exercises 94 and 95.

96.

W.B.   W.B.

97.

★ Also play 94 to 97 without slurs.

98. BOW TWISTER

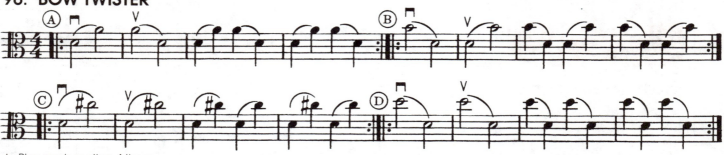

★ Play each section 4 times.

THEORY GAME

99.

★ Write in the note names.

100. GO TELL AUNT RHODIE   * Memorize   American Folk Song

W.B. W.B.

Fine

D.C. al Fine

101. IT TAKES TWO

Duet

102. SLUR THREE

★ To slur three notes, use a third of the bow for each note.

NEW IDEA

| TIE | = 4 beats | A tie is a curved line that *connects* two notes of the same pitch. Hold the note for the combined value of the two notes. |

103. HICKORY DICKORY DOCK

Traditional

★ Check your left hand position.

NEW IDEA

TIME SIGNATURE		Counting	1	2
		Alternate Counting		
$\frac{2}{4}$ = 2 beats in each measure.		$\frac{2}{4}$	𝅗𝅥	
			𝅘𝅥	𝅘𝅥
			𝅘𝅥	𝄽

104. TWO STEP MARCH

L.H.   W. B.

★ Check your bow grip often.

NEW IDEA

ARPEGGIO — An arpeggio is a broken chord. The notes of the chord are played one at a time.

105. D ARPEGGIO

★ Fingers 2 and 3 are placed ½ step apart but on different strings.

106. ARPEGGIO MARCH

★ Check the placement of your bow.

107. THE GUIDING HAND

Hatton

★ Check your bow grip often.

108. SOLO TIME

Frost

Fine

D. S. al Fine

109. PENCIL PUSHER

★ Draw in the bar lines for each section.   Be sure to notice the time signatures.

NEW NOTE

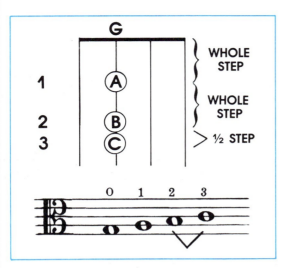

110.

111.

NEW IDEA

KEY SIGNATURE — When you see this key signature, play all the F's as F♯. This is the key signature for G Major.

112. NEW NOTES A, B AND C

113.

★ Be sure to prepare your fingers for the skips.

114.

★ Keep your fingers down where possible.

115. LONDON BRIDGE

Traditional

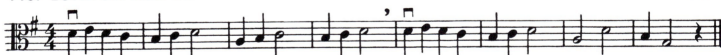

★ Check your left hand position.

116. G MAJOR SCALE

★ Refer to page 48 for other bowing and scale possibilities.

78VA

117.

118. TECHNIC TRAINER NO. 1

119. TECHNIC TRAINER NO. 2

120. TECHNIC TRAINER NO. 3

★ Special challenge. Play this line with the following bowing: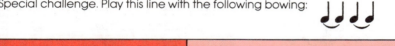

NEW IDEA

TONIC	The tonic is the keytone or first note of a scale. It is shown by I.
DOMINANT	The dominant is the fifth note of a scale. It is shown by V.

121. TONIC AND DOMINANT ARPEGGIOS

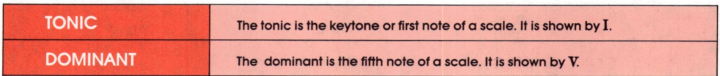

122. PETER PETER

Traditional

123. REUBEN AND RACHEL

American Folk Song

124. MELODY FOR THREE STRINGS

★ Be sure to notice the accidental (♯) in measures 9 and 12.

125. THREE STRING MADNESS

★ Special challenge. Play lines 124 and 125 with the following bowings:

a. W.B. U.H. W.B. L.H.

b. L.H. W.B. U.H. W.B.

c.   d.   e.

NEW IDEA

FIRST AND SECOND ENDINGS

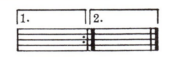

Play the first ending the first time. Then repeat the same music, skip the first ending, and play the second ending.

126. CONCERT TRIO

Frost-Trio

Fine

Fine

Fine

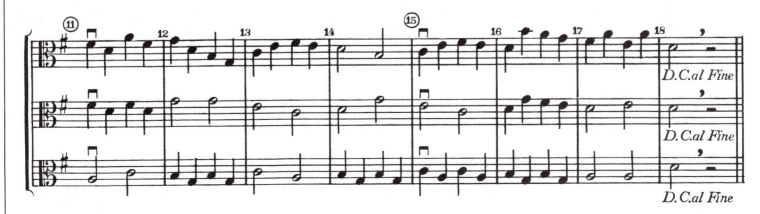

D.C.al Fine

D.C.al Fine

D.C.al Fine

NEW IDEA

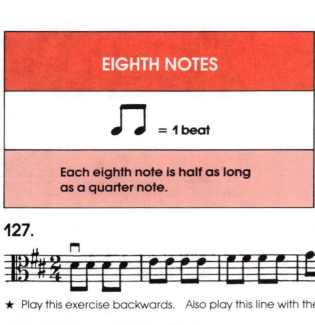

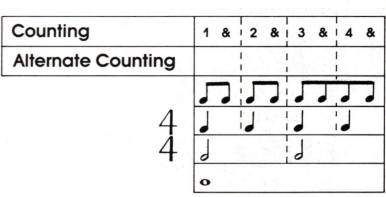

THEORY
GAME

127.

★ Play this exercise backwards.   Also play this line with the following bowings:

128. CZECH FOLK SONG

Traditional

★ Write in the counting.

129. SHE'LL BE COMIN' 'ROUND THE MOUNTAIN

American Folk Song

★ Check your left hand position.

130. LITTLE ANNIE

Czech Folk Song

L.H.   W.B.

Fine

★ Check the placement of your bow.

D.C. al Fine

THEORY
GAME

131. RHYTHM TEASER

1. Write in the counting.   2. Clap and count.   3. Play arco or pizzicato.

NEW IDEA

| TEMPOS | | Andante = moderately slow
Moderato = moderate speed
Allegro = quick and lively |

132. LONG, LONG AGO   * Memorize
Bayley

Moderato

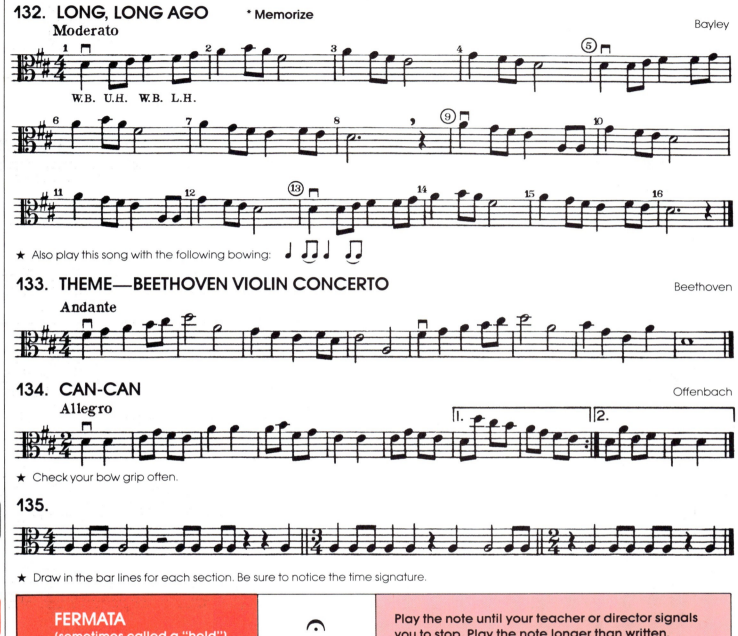

★ Also play this song with the following bowing:

133. THEME—BEETHOVEN VIOLIN CONCERTO
Beethoven

Andante

134. CAN-CAN
Offenbach

Allegro

★ Check your bow grip often.

135.

THEORY GAME

★ Draw in the bar lines for each section. Be sure to notice the time signature.

NEW IDEA

| FERMATA
(sometimes called a "hold") | ⌢ | Play the note until your teacher or director signals you to stop. Play the note longer than written. |

136. N. PAGANINI
Paganini

THEORY
GAME

137. KOOKABURRA

Australian Round

★ This round is written in the following key: _____.

THEORY
GAME

138. JOLLY OLD ST. NICK

Traditional

★ This line is written in the following key: _____.

★ Also play this line pizzicato.

NEW IDEA

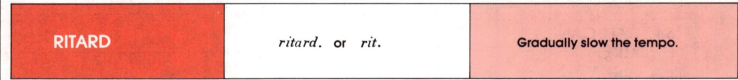

| RITARD | *ritard.* or *rit.* | Gradually slow the tempo. |

139. THE OLD WOMAN AND THE PEDDLER

English Folk Song–Ensemble

THEORY
GAME

140. RHYTHM TEASER

1. Write in the counting.   2. Clap and count.   3. Play arco or pizzicato.

NEW NOTE

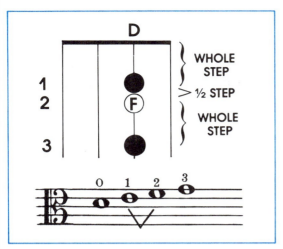

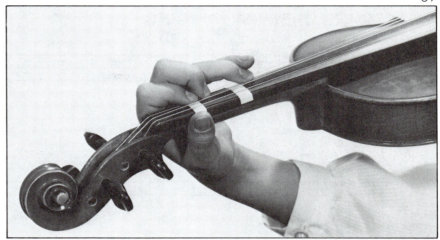

141. NEW NOTE F♮

142.

★ Stretch the 3rd finger. Be sure there is a whole step spacing between your 2nd and 3rd fingers.

143.

★ Also play this line with the following bowing: ♩ ♩ ♩

THEORY GAME

144.

★ Circle all the F♮'s in this line.

NEW IDEA

KEY SIGNATURE   When you see this key signature, play all the notes as naturals. This is the key signature for C Major.

145. FOLK SONG
Allegro

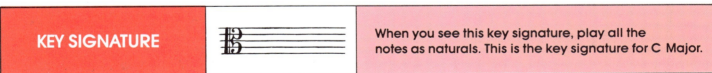

Fine   *D. C. al Fine*

146. FINGER TWISTERS

★ Play each section 4 times.

40

147. KEEP THE MUSIC RINGING

Hungarian Round

148. A TISKET A TASKET

Traditional

Moderato

149. HI-LO NO. 1

★ Pay special attention to the placement of your 2nd finger in lines 149 and 150.

150. HI-LO NO. 2

★ Also play this line with the following bowing:

THEORY GAME

151. MUSICAL ROAD SIGNS

down bow   natural sign   slur   up bow   bow lift   fermata   ½ step marking   repeat sign

★ Write in the correct musical marking in the box provided.

152. MEXICAN CLAPPING SONG—OH WHERE HAS MY LITTLE DOG GONE

Folk Songs

Allegro

153. SNAKE CHARMER

Andante

rit.

154. POSITION CHECK

Right Hand	Left Hand	Playing Position
☐ Thumb bent	☐ Wrist straight	☐ Instrument held up
☐ Little finger curved	☐ Elbow under	☐ Sitting up properly
		☐ Straight bow stroke

Have your teacher check your position.   **Place an X in the box for each item that is correct in your playing.**

NEW NOTE

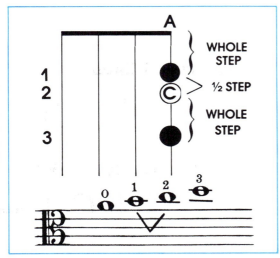

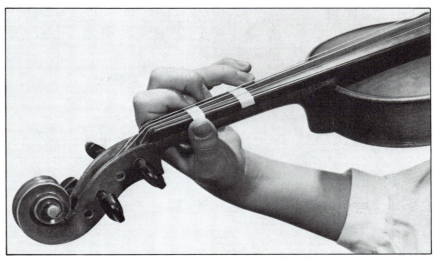

155. NEW NOTE C♮

156.

157. SOME FOLKS DO

Foster

158.

159. BOW TWISTER

160. TECHNIC TRAINER

161. FINGER TWISTER

★ Play each section 4 times.

NEW IDEA

DYNAMICS	f	= *forte*	= Loud
	mf	= *mezzo forte*	= Medium loud
	p	= *piano*	= Soft

162. CANON

Tallis

163. FRENCH FOLK SONG * Memorize

★ Be sure to use good bow division.

164. BRIDGE AT AVIGNON

French Folk Song

165. THERE'S MUSIC IN THE AIR

Root-Ensemble

THEORY GAME

166. FINGERING REVIEW

① Write in the fingering, either H2 or L2, under each note.
② In the fingering chart above, write the name of the note that is played at the place of each circle.

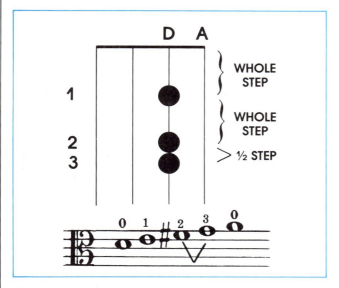

167. NEW NOTES F♯ AND G

168. NEW NOTE A

169. TECHNIC TRAINER

170. G MAJOR SCALE WITH BROKEN THIRDS

Also play this exercise substituting the correct number of eighth notes for each written note:

★ Refer to page 48 for other bowing and scale possibilities.

171. ARPEGGIO FUN

★ Also play this song slurring three quarter notes as follows:

THEORY GAME

172. WHEN LOVE IS KIND

Irish Folk Song

★ This line is written in the following key:_____.

173. SAINTS

Traditional

THEORY GAME

174. SKIP TO MY LOU

American Folk Song

★ This line is written in the following key._____.

175. SHEPHERD'S HEY

English Folk Song

NEW NOTES

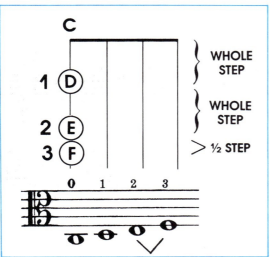

176. NEW NOTES C, D AND E (violas and cellos play on their C string)

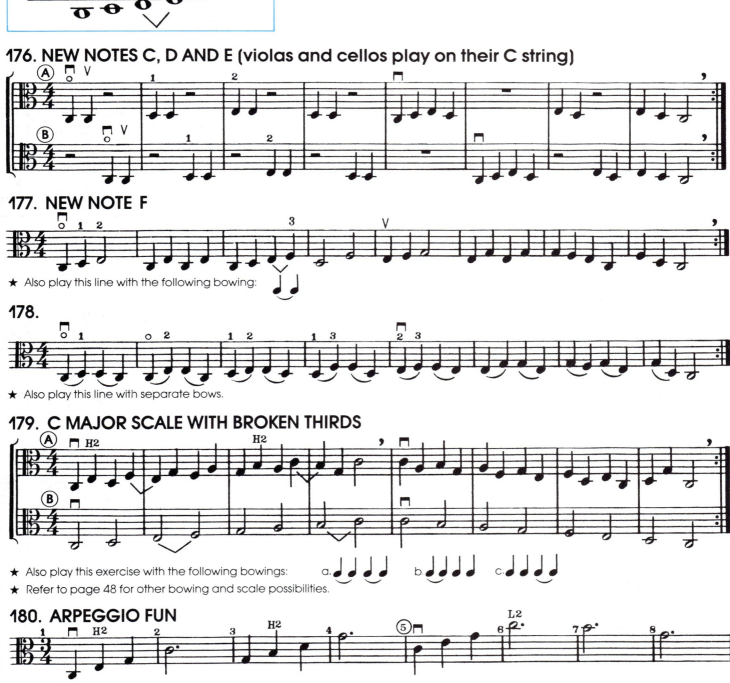

177. NEW NOTE F

★ Also play this line with the following bowing:

178.

★ Also play this line with separate bows.

179. C MAJOR SCALE WITH BROKEN THIRDS

★ Also play this exercise with the following bowings: a. b. c.

★ Refer to page 48 for other bowing and scale possibilities.

180. ARPEGGIO FUN

★ Also play this line slurring the three quarter notes:

THEORY GAME

181. DUET IN TWO KEYS

Frost-Duet

1. The A part is written in the following key:_____.

2. The B part is written in the following key:_____.

NEW IDEA

| THEME AND VARIATIONS | A simple tune followed by the same tune with changes. |

182. THEME AND VARIATIONS

Theme

Anderson

mf

Fine

Variation 1

f

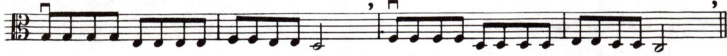

Variation 2

p

Variation 3

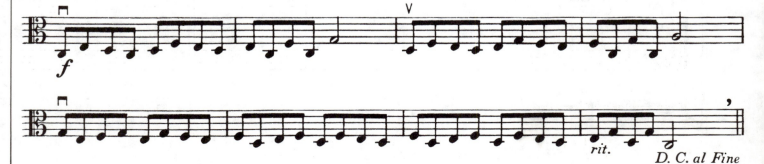

f

rit.

D. C. al Fine

D.C. AL CODA

D.C. AL CODA	*D. C.* (Da Capo) = to the beginning *al Coda* = to Coda *Coda* = ending

When you see the *D. C. al Coda* go back to the beginning.
When you come to the ⊕ (Coda sign) skip to the Coda.

183. HAPPY BLUES
Frost

184. JAZZ FEATURE
Anderson

Rhythm patterns for the B part:
★ Play pizzicato.

78VA

TECHNIC DEVELOPMENT

1. D MAJOR SCALE

2. D MAJOR BROKEN THIRDS

3. G MAJOR SCALE

4. G MAJOR BROKEN THIRDS

5. C MAJOR SCALE

6. C MAJOR BROKEN THIRDS

Play the scales and broken thirds with the rhythms and bowings listed below. Be sure to play these rhythms and bowings with good bow division.

Bow Divisions:

Whole Bow = W. B.   Upper Half = U. H.   Lower Half = L. H.   Middle = M.

8. Slur 4 notes   16. Slur 2 notes   24. Slur 3 notes